I0483885

Real Ways to Make Money from Home

Start Making Money Now

Adeline Ganley

FrugalFanatic.com

Real Ways to Make Money from Home
© Copyright 2015 Adeline Ganley

FrugalFanatic.com

All Rights Reserved. No part of this publication may be reproduced, stored in a retrieval system, or transmitted in any form – to include: electronic transmissions, photocopies, or recordings of any kind – without prior written permission of the authors.

Cover design by
JD Havrilla | jdhavrilla.com

Indie Publishing Services by
Melinda Martin of TheHelpyHelper.com

(She works from home!)

TOPICS

WHAT OTHERS ARE SAYING:

"I've only been blogging for 14 months now, and I make full time income blogging as a single, stay at home mom. Much of my success I credit to Addi. She has a wealth of knowledge and knows Google Analytics better than anyone else I know. She loves figuring out what makes a blog successful and pinpoints ways to help. She is highly creative and knows her stuff inside and out. She is, however, not a trumpet-blowing person, so you'll just have to trust that she is awesome and has the stats to prove it. I highly recommend hiring Addi to help you with your blog. I do not honestly believe I would not be where I am today without her. She is an amazing person, and I'm honored to get to call her a friend." -Sarah, SarahTitus.com

"Frugal Fanatic has helped me to find small ways to save money and start to get out of debt. I frequently check this blog to learn how I can stretch my budget and also learn new ways to make money online." -Anonymous

ABOUT THE AUTHOR

Addi is a mom, wife, blogger and founder of FrugalFanatic.com. Since launching in 2011, her site has allowed her to help teach people how to live a frugal lifestyle while maintaining a tight budget. She loves showing her readers how they can make money from home without having to work a typical nine to five job. Her passion is to raise her children at home while still earning a full-time income to help support her family. Addi lives in Pittsburgh, Pennsylvania with her husband and three boys.

Frugal Fanatic came about as a way to help show people how they can save money in their every day lives. Since then it has grown into a popular personal finance blog while also showing people how they can work from home and earn a full-time income. Making money from home takes time and dedication. It is not a one-time thing. Being able to find multiple sources to create passive income is key.

Frugal Fanatic covers topics that include frugal living, work from home jobs, affiliate marketing, personal finance tips, side jobs, blogging revenue and various other topics. Stay connected with Frugal Fanatic on Facebook, Twitter, Pinterest and join the weekly newsletter so you can receive updates directly to your inbox.

INTRODUCTION

I am so excited to share with you some tried and true real ways to make money from home. Whether you are a stay at home mom looking for extra income or work full-time outside of the home but would love to supplement your income, then I have some awesome options for you to learn about. Within each section of this book, I will go into detail about how to make these work at home jobs work for you.

No matter what your skill set may be, I hope to give you some great pointers and tips on beginning your new life working from home.

Often times, people only consider having a normal nine to five job with the option to work from home. But there are a lot of ways that you can earn a full-time income from your home without having to even work forty hours a week.

The purpose of *Real Ways To Make Money From Home* is to teach you about all the different possibilities of earning an income from home. I never believed that I could make real money working from home while still raising my children. Now that I make a full-time income I know that it is possible. With the right job and dedication you can do it too.

Even though every work from home job in this book may not fit with your lifestyle or interests I wanted to show you the various options available to earn money from home. Many people are not aware of the how they can earn money their particular skills or expertise.

I would recommend starting with one of the jobs in this book and figure out if it fits well with you. Do not jump right in and try everything because it will be very overwhelming. Plus, it would not give you the time to really focus on one job, which could lead to failure or burnout.

My hope is that you will learn about various new job opportunities as you read this book so that you too can make money from home.

Are you ready to work from home?

ONLINE SURVEYS

In this digital age we live in, online money making schemes are common. When many people hear the words "make money doing surveys" they hesitate and think that it is a scam. Yes, there are a lot of scams, but there are some great options to still make money from home.

There are legitimate ways to make money taking online surveys, however these are not get rich quick schemes and often times do not provide a full time income. They do however give you an easy method of making money at home quickly, safely and legally.

Whenever I started looking for ways to make some extra money online, surveys were one of the first options I turned to. Not only are surveys one of the easiest ways to get started they are simple to do in your spare time. I was surprised when I first started completing online surveys because I was able to quickly make an extra fifty dollars each month. Then, I really started to try other companies and quickly made more each month.

Online surveys will often times have the option for product sampling and rewards programs. Not all of them will give you the option to cash out for each survey you complete.

Online survey sites are a dime a dozen. There are a handful I will share with you that are legitimate and will pay you money, but you have to understand how they work and what to look for. Not only can you earn money from website surveys, but there are now dozens of smart phone apps that are available to earn rewards with as well. When it comes to real ways to make money from home, these are some of the best places to start because there are no investments and anyone can do them. Plus, online surveys give you the freedom to make money in your spare time.

In this section I will go into detail of what each of these are, what to expect, and how much money you can to expect from them. I will help you weed out the scams, learn how to make real legitimate money taking surveys and show you which rewards programs to use to supplement your income.

HOW TO MAKE MONEY WITH ONLINE SURVEYS

When you first start looking at online survey sites, you will see dozens of options. Within those options you will find three different types of sites.

- **Cash payout via check or Paypal.** These sites will pay you when you complete qualifying surveys. You will need meet their payout threshold and then you will be paid via a check mailed to your home, direct deposit in your bank account or a deposit into your Paypal account. These are the most desirable sites to work with because it is the easiest way to get paid.

- **Gift card payout via Amazon, Target or other mass retailers.** Some sites will reward you with points to be redeemed in their onsite rewards shop where you have the option to buy gift cards or merchandise with your accumulate rewards points. These are great for those who want to save up money for things like buying gifts, going on vacation or holiday spending. Gift cards are easy to store until use and seem to last longer for some.

- **Rewards points used for onsite sweepstakes.** These sites are common, but not recommend for frequent use. Completing surveys on these sites will reward you with points that are then converted into sweepstakes entries on their site. With no guaranteed payout for your effort, they are a gamble and not a favorite of mine to be a part of.

When you begin looking at survey sites, you'll want to take a look at their payment options and payout threshold. This will become important as you try to meet financial goals later on.

To really make the most of your experience working from home online survey sites, you will need to have some organization. While this is not a regular job that requires set hours or days of work, it is something you want to take seriously if you plan to make money from it. To become successful, I have some basic tips that will help keep you on track.

- **Use multiple sites.** Although the majority of survey sites will offer the same or similar surveys, it is a good idea to use multiple sites to up your chances of qualifying for surveys to complete. Some will payout at higher rates while others will be given different demographics to cover. It is better to have more options since you will not get accepted foe every survey.

- **Keep good records.** This is really important when it comes to knowing what these sites owe you. Some will credit your account as soon as the survey is submitted. Others however will wait to submit until the survey has been reviewed. Make notes of what you complete and how much is owed to you for each survey. Also, make sure to make notes on when you request a payout so you know when to expect it to arrive in your bank or Paypal account. This is especially good if you start working with multiple survey sites.

- **Update your demographics regularly.** This is really important. You are approved for surveys according to your demographics like age, race, living situation or geographical location. Update regularly with any changes so that you are offered opportunities that fit your demographics.

These tips will help to keep you on track with online survey sites you choose to work with. Not only will you know what you are making, but when to expect to see it in your bank account.

Another thing to consider when utilizing online survey sites as a source of work at home income is consistency. Many of these sites look at what surveys you should be offered according to how often you check in and take surveys on their site.

- **Set up a surveys only email account.** This is really important to keep your inbox clean and easy to organize. Before you get started with any online survey company I recommend opening a new email account that will only be used for completing surveys. This gives you one location to look easily and quickly to find out what new survey are open to you. Most companies offer quick daily surveys that you have the option to complete, so having them together one email makes it much easier. Plus, you may be receiving multiple emails a day and do not want all of those to be mixed in with your personal emails.

- **Check the sites not just your emails.** You will often receive mail invitations to take surveys that are new on their site. However, you want to also log into the site itself to check regularly. Sometimes there are specific items that will not show up in your email that you could miss out on if you do not check the sites regularly, which leads me to the next tip.

- **Check in to each site regularly.** Even if you cannot do so daily, make a routine of checking into sites even when you have not received emails with new opportunities. Staying active with regular logins will show them you are interested so they keep your account on their list to notify of new opportunities.

Focusing on consistency will help you to make more money with online surveys. There will be sites where you find yourself being turned down for surveys, and others where you get tons of offers. You need to check all sites regularly as these cycles do change depending on what is offered to them.

When it comes to the actual money made from a survey company, the amount varies from company to company. You will see payouts as low as $.05 per survey and up to $150 per survey. These ranges are giant and can be frustrating when you are really wanting to see big numbers in your accounts. You have to understand that different companies pay out at different rates and it depends on how extensive the survey may be. You also have to accept that you must build consistency with companies before they will offer you higher payout opportunities.

- **Never pay to participate in a survey site.** If a survey site requires a monthly or annual fee to participate I would stay away. Be cautious of these companies because you should never have to pay to participate on a survey site. However, there are trustworthy sites that offer review opportunities that require an up front purchase of a product or service. There are situations that you will need to weigh individually to make sure they are for you. Some are satellite or cell phone contracts, but others have simply been a weekend carpet cleaning rental. These will require up front purchase, but you will be reimbursed for the purchase as well as a significant amount for your post purchase survey.

- **Do all surveys that are open to you no matter how low the pay.** These will add up faster than you think. Completing ten very short (3-5 question) surveys at $.50 each is still $5.00 and can be completed in a matter of minutes.

If you have decided to include online surveys in your at home money making regiment, you must accept and realize that they are not going to provide you with a full time income. Surveys are a great way to supplement your income with some easy money. You can make enough money each year to pay for things like holiday gifts, weekend getaways or your weekly manicure. I love saving this extra money for special occasions.

MY RECOMMENDED SURVEY SITES

Online survey sites change frequently so be sure to reach each one before getting started so that you fully understand what you are getting into. Also, another tip is to make sure you designate time to complete each survey. In the past, I was given a pre-survey questionnaire to see if I qualified. I was accepted and then immediately sent right into the survey. Well, this particular survey took twenty minutes to complete. I did not end up having enough time and I had to stop half way through. Needless to say you do not get paid for a half completed survey.

Pinecone Research: This is a great group to go with that does tons of surveys for all demographics. They typically offer $3-$5 per survey, but occasionally will have larger opportunities offered. They are especially popular as they have specific surveys for Hispanics, African Americans and Men as well.

InboxDollars: This company will pay you to read emails, take surveys online, play games and even go shopping. Plus, new enrollees receive $5 just for joining with InboxDollars.

Vindale Research: Vindale has been a standard in online surveys for years. They offer a wide variety of surveys that payout for as low as $.35 but as high as $150. This site also offers regular opportunities to review a service or product in exchange for reimbursement and stipend. The payout is higher than others and is a great place to begin and build up income slowly.

Even though it may seem like a lot of information to get started working from home by completing surveys, it is quite easy. Once you get into a routine and understand each company you will be on your way to making some extra cash.

VIRTUAL ASSISTANT

Another amazing way to make money from home is to become a virtual assistant. This job is one that can cover literally dozens of fields of expertise while being flexible to your needs. Virtual assistance has become a very popular method of working from home that is picking up speed in many online communities. In this section, I hope to give you some solid tips on how to begin working from home as a virtual assistant, how you can make money and even what you will need to charge your clients.

A virtual assistant is someone who does a job remotely or online. These can be everything from a personal assistant who schedules appointments, answers emails and organizes a to-do list, to someone who ghostwrites for a blog or schedules social media for businesses. There are numerous ways to be a virtual assistant, but the goal is to assist an individual or business in a way that they need while working from home at your convenience.

Why would this be beneficial to you? Being a virtual assistant allows you to use talents or skills you already possess. It also allows you to work within a flexible schedule around your duties at home. Additionally, it gives you the freedom to run your business the way you wish. While you will be working for clients, you can set your standard rates of pay and times you will be available.

For parents of young children, or those who might have physical disabilities that make being in an office difficult, becoming a virtual assistant is an excellent choice.

WHAT DOES A VIRTUAL ASSISTANT DO?

The jobs of a virtual assistant vary from person to person. That is what makes this one of the largest trending work at home positions of the last few years. Not only can those who are great with spreadsheets and getting organized be virtual assistants, so can graphic designers, freelance writers, social media managers and even people who like to cook at home. What you do virtually for another person or business varies greatly and is totally up to you.

Here are some of the most common types of virtual assistants:

- Social Media Marketer

- Online Appointment Scheduler

- Email Organization (Respond, Send New and Organize existing)

- Website Content Organization

- Graphic Design

- Blog/Content Promotion

- Create Slideshows, Spreadsheets and other paperwork needed for business

- Assist blog owners in content creation and website maintenance duties

- Website Design

- Streamline business websites for SEO and website search engine results

- Photography

- Maintain business or brand blogs

- Paralegal assistant

- Medical office scheduler

- Real Estate scheduler and assistant

This list is not inclusive, but gives you a simple idea of some of the tasks that qualified virtual assistants can do for a business. Even if you have never considered becoming a virtual assistant, you may see things on this list that you know you are qualified to complete. Whether you have experience or are an expert your services are valuable and you can be paid for various jobs.

Virtual assistants have made a name for themselves in the work at home industry because of their versatility. Not only are there many different kinds of VA's as they are often called, but they are becoming a much more sought after part of the business community.

To become a successful virtual assistant, you must decide what skill sets you possess that could be used by a business, blogger, website or even small business in your community. Think about your past work experiences. Did you work in an office and utilize things like spreadsheets, presentations or scheduling appointments? Perhaps you are a former real estate agent who could assist with paperwork, scheduling appointments or even submitting listings to websites. There are a multitude of places for you to work virtually for other businesses.

WHERE TO ADVERTISE YOURSELF AS A VIRTUAL ASSISTANT

Knowing how to market your virtual assistant business is the key to success. Unlike some other work at home businesses, this one will require you putting forth a considerable effort to land a job.

Local Community: You can easily advertise your virtual assistant business to your local community simply by creating a flyer or business cards to share with local businesses that you feel you could help.

Facebook Virtual Assistant Groups: Simply search for the term Virtual Assistant or VA on Facebook or LinkedIn and you will find tons of great groups and pages that will help connect you to clients. Often times you can submit what types of jobs you are capable of doing in these groups and will immediately get responses. Also, you will find listings for people who are seeking particular jobs that you can comment and apply for directly on Facebook. This is an excellent place to start. I hire a lot of VA's through Facebook groups and there are jobs posted daily. One good example that you may not have considered with VA jobs is cooking and photographing recipes that you make at home. Blogs are always seeking high quality recipes and photos to post on their website. Normally you can be paid anywhere from $25 to $50 for each unique recipe. This is a great option for anyone who loves to cook or bake.

Elance, Odesk or Fiverr: All three of these sites are perfect for posting an online resume, bidding on jobs or offering services at varying rates of pay. They also offer an insight into what others are offering so you can check out your competition before setting up a job listing.

HOW TO BE AN EFFECTIVE VIRTUAL ASSISTANT

The most important things to remember as you work to become an effective virtual assistant are to be organized, persistent, and professional. Just because you are working from home does not mean you are not a professional. If you plan to succeed, you must take this business seriously.

Things you'll need to be a good virtual assistant:

- Quality reliable Internet connection

- Up to date reliable computer

- Calendar and organized method of keeping up with your assignments

- Dedicated business email account and potentially phone number

- Organized schedule

These are simple things that will help you to succeed as a virtual assistant. Remember that this job is one that depends on your performance with your clients to continue getting more referrals. Once you gain a few clients, you will be able to create a great website with testimonials to send your potential clients to. Remember that doing a quality job will result in you finding more clients to help build your business and work from home income.

You may need to offer some of your services for free or extremely cheap when you are first starting out so that you can have the experience to provide for future clients.

One of the best aspects about being a VA is you may start out part-time doing random jobs for several clients and then land a full-time job with one client.

Being a virtual assistant allows you to set your prices and you normally get paid per job.

FREELANCE WRITING
& GHOST WRITING

For those who have a knack with words, there are tons of opportunities online to make money as a freelance writer or even a ghost writer. This is a business that can be lucrative when you find the right clients, but can also be very difficult to get into. For most who find success in the writing world, they do so by building their own website or blog, writing eBooks and selling themselves on Amazon, or finding one client that really puts them to work.

The term freelance writing has often received a poor reputation because it can be one of the most difficult ways for a talented writer to earn a living. However, there are a multitude of ways to get your talent out there in front of others and make a paycheck in the process. Many people view a freelance writer differently than a ghost writer. In my experience, a freelance writer will write about topics they enjoy and are very knowledgeable about. Sometimes they will receive credit for their work with their name listed in the article while ghost writes normally write on a provided topic given to them from a client. The client will then use the article as their own as if they wrote it themselves. A ghost writer does not get credit for their work, but they are often times paid more since a blogger or website is buying the rights to their work and taking credit for it.

Successful freelance writers and ghost writers know that marketing yourself and having quality testimonials on your resume are the key to success. Simply submitting an article to your favorite online publication is not enough to land the next big thing. There are tons of connections needed to make sure you not only have that one hit article or story, but dozens in the future. This is one of the most fun ways to make money working from home, but also one that requires the most work. For those who are willing to put in long hours for lower pay, it is a great way to make income from home while writing about things you love and are knowledgeable and passionate about. I know that may sound odd because who wants to work more for less money, but writing can be a hobby and is often used as an outlet to share thoughts and ideas that people enjoy doing. So why not get paid for it if you fit into this category.

WHERE TO MARKET YOURSELF AS A WRITER

Just because you have written a wonderful, informative, or witty article does not mean that it is going to be seen unless you put yourself out there in the right forums. To begin there are a few things you need to do to ensure you have a professional appearance.

Brand yourself: Build a website for yourself, get a custom email and grab your own social media pages using your name or pen name. I will focus more on creating a blog in the next section. It may seem like an overwhelming task, but setting up a basic blog is easy and can be done in a few simple steps.

Join author groups on social media: Facebook and LinkedIn provide a ton of excellent groups for freelance writers. Not only will you find information on building better content in these groups, you will often find great opportunities to write for clients on a regular basis.

Join Elance, Odesk & Fiverr: I have mentioned these sites before for other work at home opportunities, but they are some of the best places to look for work as a freelance writer. From simple short blog post creation to lengthy articles or tutorials these have great opportunities for you to bid or submit your work.

Post to About.com, Squidoo or EHow: These sites offer great opportunities for you to submit your articles on varying subjects.

Post articles to your own blog: Making money from a blog is another great way to work from home we will cover later, but works excellently for writers.

Submit to local print publications: Your local newspaper, city magazine or state magazine are great places to submit work.

Work for bloggers as content creators: Many popular blogs hire freelance and/or ghost writers to create content about a multitude of subjects. This can be everything from mommy blogger articles to technology reviews. I have hired a lot of freelance writers to write articles for my blog. It is an excellent way to get a fresh perspective on topics I normally post about as well as having new contributors on my blog.

Write eBooks for yourself or others: Many individuals hire ghost writers to complete eBooks for them to sell on their websites or even sites like Amazon, Goodreads or Barnes & Noble. You can offer this as a service to others, or write for yourself and submit to Amazon and sell for a low price.

HOW TO GET NOTICED AS A WRITER

Getting the attention of people who are reading your articles, blog posts or even your eBooks is not an easy task. Even the most brilliant authors in years past have struggled to have their work viewed. This is one case where it sometimes can be an issue of knowing the right person at the right time. Regardless, there are some great ways to make sure your content gets seen and is purchased by potential clients.

- **Write about current needs or upcoming technology.** Look at current trends and write about things that are trending, seasonal or are part of upcoming technology or entertainment releases.

- **Appeal to unique target audiences.** Sometimes the oddball groups or niches are the best to target for consistent traffic. Smaller groups may not seem like they will bring enough traffic, but since there are fewer articles about their niche, you'll find higher rate of return for your effort.

- **Educate yourself on formats and search engine optimization (SEO).** Learning about keywords, SEO, and verbiage in online articles can increase views to your work since most bloggers are looking to purchase articles that are SEO optimized.

- **Build testimonials to update on your resume for potential clients.** Always ask for testimonials of any company that you work for to add to your website or resume.

- **Start small and upsell as you grow.** Some hesitate to work with sites like Fiverr that pay low fees, but it is a great way to build a client base and get experience.

Becoming a successful freelance writer or ghost writer can happen to those who are willing to work hard. If you have a natural talent with words, this could easily become one of the best ways for you to make money from home. Topics to write about are endless, and do not have to center around fiction as some would think. Freelance writing and ghost writing are common place in many arenas online and in print publications.

Hone your skills and begin submitting your work to various online and print publications. In time you will find yourself making a steady income publishing written work on various websites, blogs and magazines.

It is hard to pinpoint exactly how much money you can make as a freelance or ghost writer. Most of the time people pay by the length of the article. The majority of jobs I have seen offer $15 to $40 for a 300 - 500 word article. So, depending on how many you can write in a month you can earn great money working from home as a freelance writer or offering ghost writing services.

Like any other job, there are always downsides. Many clients that you work with will have high demands and short deadlines. You may be asked for several revisions and be required to submit changes quickly. I would advise to take the time to figure out all of the expectations and demands before taking on any freelance writing job.

BLOGGING

One of the most popular ways to make money from home in recent years has been blogging. Many interviews over the last few years have shown that bloggers can successfully make upwards of $75,000 per year from their website. While that is on the high end for the average blogger, it is even possible to make a six figure income if you work hard and are diligent. Many people ask how you can make money writing about things like potty training tips or the latest video game release, and that is what this chapter is going to help you to understand. Not only will I lay out the simple methods of making money from a blog I will give you some basic tips on starting a blog.

Blogs are not just for mommies, foodies or crafters. A blog can be used for a multitude of purposes and are often used by brands to help showcase their products. Whether you are someone who is single and has no desire to blog about kids, diapers and daily life, or a fitness guru who wants to share tips on workouts and protein shakes there is always room in the blogosphere for your commentary and thoughts.

Blogs make money in various ways such as advertisements, ebooks, sponsorships, text links, freelance writing, merchandise sales and a handful of other ways. Every blog makes money differently because of their content, audience, traffic, goals and many other factors. No matter what your preferences is or niche may be, there are always ways to monetize your blog. While I will share simple information on how to make money from blogging, you will need to research things like how to build traffic to your site, learning how to utilize social media and even simple formatting methods that make your site an easier read for your followers. There are a lot of factors that play into the success of a blog.

HOW TO START A BLOG

Before you worry about building a website or finding ads to make money, you really need to consider what type of blog you want to have. There is literally a place for everything on the Internet, and that means your blog can be about whatever you want it to be.

Popular blog topics:

- Mommy, parenting and kids

- Health & fitness

- Recipes

- Deals and savings

- Entertainment (general & genre specific – movies, video games, music, etc.)

- Fashion (makeup, clothing, kids fashion, women's fashion, men's fashion and plus size fashion)

- DIY & Crafts

- Organization and daily life tips

- Personal Finance blogs

Every blog is a little bit different, and no two blogs are going to present topics identically. While layouts, styles and even some articles may be similar there is no set standard to blogging that you must follow. While there are many things you need to do to be professional as a blogger, it does not always matter what your website looks like or how many ads you have on it.

HOW TO MAKE MONEY FROM YOUR BLOG

When I first started blogging I was clueless. I did not even know that making money was a possibility. Now that I earn a full-time income I know that it is possible to work from home blogging and that my earnings potential is endless. There is no single answer to the question of how you can make money from your blog. There are multiple ways to make money blogging that I will briefly cover that you can consider doing once you have a blog up and running. Remember that you will have to post content as well as work on building traffic via social media, search engine optimization and email connections. Even though you are able to work from home, blogging tasks never end. It is a full-time job in itself especially if you want it to be your main source of income.

Many bloggers will tell you that it takes years to make money blogging, but I have proven that wrong. I made money in my first month of blogging. Although it was only enough to buy a couple packs of gum it was still money. Within a few months I was making a couple hundred dollars. At that time I had no idea what I was doing and wish I did because I know that I wasted a lot of time and could have made much, much more money. Here are a few options to make money on your blog.

Advertisement: Many blogs offer ad space to both companies and other websites or blogs on their site. Depending on your blog traffic and following, you may be able to charge a flat fee monthly or annually to have ads placed in your sidebar, header or other areas of your site.

You can also consider pay per click ads. These usually come in the form of ads generated by companies like Adsense, Glam, Media.net, and other pay per click ad networks. These rotating ads will be placed in your header, footer, sidebars and even within your blog posts themselves. Your income from these ads will vary according to traffic to your site and agreed upon payment per click from advertisers. This is one of the easiest way to monetize your blog.

Review products and posts: Many blogs find themselves able to receive products and opportunities in exchange for a review on their site and social media. While this does not always include cash payment, it does often include product or service that is given to you in exchange for your written review. For many individuals the free product is more than enough compensation. From free food to kids' toys and games or even vacations for larger blogs and audiences, these opportunities can be very lucrative. While you may not see cash in your pocket to pay bills, it still is income of sorts. But, be cautious with these companies because they often expect a lot of work for such a small ticket item in return. You need to consider the time and effort you put into the post and promoting it. Since you will not be receiving a cash payment the item would need to be an appropriate value equal the amount you need to be paid for the post.

Sponsored Posts: There are a multitude of companies that work together with bloggers to promote brands and businesses. These companies provide you with sponsored post opportunities. This means you would write a blog post, create a craft or even develop a recipe featuring the brand product and you promote it on your blog and social media in exchange for a lump sum payment, or occasionally a pay per click payment on links or ads within the post.

Working with brands is a great way to increase your earnings while still writing about topics you love. Be sure to check out the company you are partnering with for the post. You need to be able to post about a company that you trust and think would be a great fit for your blog and audience since you are potentially recommending them. Even though you may want to take the money for a sponsored post you need to make sure it fits well with your site otherwise your readers will be confused as to why you are posting about something completely unrelated to your blog.

You can obtain sponsored posts by pitching companies yourself or using networks like Izea, Tap Influence, Pollinate Media or Clever Girls.

Affiliate Links: There are thousands of websites that will allow you to link out to their products and earn a commission on any purchases made through your link. Some of the most common companies are Amazon, Share A Sale, Commission Junction and Linkshare. These are a great place to start when looking to make money from your blog. When it comes to making money with affiliate links you want to make sure it fits organically within in a post and not just a placed link. Your readers will trust you and know when you are just trying to sell a product or when you are genuinely recommending something for them to use.

While making money from blogging is a possibility, it does require a lot of work and effort on your part. There are a multitude of ways to make a blog a great source of passive income for your budget. Even though I cannot give you an exact dollar amount that bloggers make I can tell you that a six figure income is possible. It all depends on the amount of time and dedication you put into blogging. It does become a business and like any business you have to work at it for it to grow and be successful.

PHOTOGRAPHY

If you often find yourself behind the lens of the camera as you look for ways to make money from home, you are in luck. One of the most popular ways to earn a living is to become a photographer. While this is something that requires skill and equipment, it is also something that can be managed with some training and practice. Many individuals have a natural eye for beauty through a lens, but even those with no experience can learn and manage to have a successful photography business. Photography is a wonderful way to work from home. It allows you the freedom to work as much or as little as you want. Even though you cannot do this job completely at home it is an awesome option to earn a full-time income.

In this section I will look at some basic types of photography as well as how to market yourself, but first I want to talk about what is really important to begin. Having the right tools for the job really is very important. It is not about having the latest and greatest DSLR, but about knowing how to use the tools you have at hand.

Professional photographers take years to educate themselves on technique, equipment, lighting and even the processing methods available. For most at home photographers these days, the art of truly learning photography is gone. However, you can spend time learning and educating yourself for free online. You may even be able to find a local photographer who will work with you and tutor you on skill, lighting and how to utilize your camera.

Without a doubt, pricey cameras give you more tools and a sharp image with less effort, but you can take a simple $100 camera and create a phenomenal picture to share when you know how to utilize your camera. You do the research and education part, and I will direct you on how to take that skill and market it in your community and online to make money.

WHERE CAN YOU MAKE MONEY WITH PHOTOGRAPHY?

When you pick up your camera and grab that perfect picture, you know you can use it to make money, but where do you even begin? I am going to outline a few of the most common ways to take your skill behind the lens and turn it into a steady source of work from home income.

- **Local portrait photography.** Many new photographers create a local following by doing simple portrait and family photography in their local community. This can range from basic portraits, weddings, senior portraits, family portraits or annual holiday pictures for cards. This also includes things like doing photography for local daycares, church directories or even small business office photography for records or marketing.

- **Local newspaper action photography.** Many local newspapers, magazines and print publications hire photographers to handle their action shots as needed in the community.

- **Stock photos.** There are dozens of websites that sell stock photos to be used by individuals for websites, advertising and more. Quality images can be sold on these sites for a fee per use. Food and craft photography as well as life events, general architecture, outdoor shots and various images of all styles are all needed on a regular basis. Even though you can sell your stock photos online there is a lot of competition on these websites. It is a great place to start but you need to take high quality photos. Before you start I recommend taking a look at sires like iStock and BigStock to see what other kinds of photos are selling.

HOW TO MARKET YOURSELF AS A PHOTOGRAPHER

Once you have acquired a decent camera and learned all the tricks of the trade, you need to start marketing yourself for the jobs I mentioned on the last page. There are numerous ways to go about getting your name out in the community, but it will begin with creating a portfolio of your images so others can see them.

- Take pictures of local landmarks, buildings and your own family.

- Offer a free session to friends or neighbors.

Building your portfolio is low cost to you. It simply requires your time and perhaps a few volunteers willing to be in your images. This time gives you the chance to work out your technique, play with editing in different programs and learn more about the workings of your camera.

Next you will want to share those images from your portfolio in areas that will grab the attention of potential customers.

- Create business social media pages, as well as a simple website for information. This is a great place to show off the amazing pictures you have taken to potential clients.

- Place an ad in your local newspaper or city magazine.

- Share your information in local Facebook Swap Shop groups.

- Offer services on sites like Odesk, Elance and Fiverr.

- Contact friends who may need stock images for their websites, blogs or business needs.

Photography can be a wonderful business with relatively low start-up costs, and tons of opportunities to make money around your own flexible schedule. Working from home making real money as a photographer is not just a dream, but can become a reality for many individuals.

Spend plenty of time reading about your camera and its settings. Take free online photography classes, or watch videos online that include tips and information on how to make the most of lighting and editing programs. Educating yourself and practicing is the most important part of becoming a photographer. You cannot simply point and click to create a great photograph. I would recommend looking for local photography courses to take if you are a hands-on learner.

This is just another great way you can easily make money from home. Many artistic and creative individuals love using their talent for imagery as a means to create beautiful photographs that can be shared while still earning an income.

Even though this will take time to build there is a lot of potential to have your own photography business to make money from home.

I know a lot of stay at home moms that started taking pictures as a hobby and slowly built up a list of clients. They have now made their passion a business and shoot weddings, newborn photos and a variety of other events in their spare time. This option may not be for everyone but it is definitely something to consider if you love taking pictures.

GRAPHIC DESIGN

In this section, I will look at some of the ways you can make money from home doing graphic design work. This is one instance where skill and a complete understanding of the medium is necessary for success. Learning how to do graphic design is not something you pick up overnight. It is a skill that will require a significant amount of practice, education, and understanding of the programs involved. To be ultimately successful with this, you must possess some knowledge already – or be willing to put the time, money and energy into learning how to create on your own. One of the best aspects of graphic design work is that you get to show off your talents and get paid for them while you complete the work in the comforts of your home.

Graphic design is something that has become a popular job in the last few decades. Using various computer programs, you can manipulate images to change their appearance, or you can create entirely new images all your own. This has been used for everything from making cartoons and animated films, to creating the logo that is on the front of this book. Graphic design can be used for a multitude of things and can become something very profitable to you.

If you already have a knack for graphic design or have a distinct interest and are willing to put in the time and money to learn more, this section will give you some fun and new ways to make money online or even in your local community. This will require some financial investment for a quality computer, education and software to complete tasks. Make sure when setting out on this journey that the investment is something you are willing and able to make for a future of successful work at home business experience.

HOW TO MAKE MONEY AS A GRAPHIC DESIGNER

Just because you can create beautiful images does not mean that you are going to have people who know that. You must market yourself well in multiple areas to become truly successful. For those who want to take this to a much larger level and career (perhaps even the teen wanting to create graphics for movies, video games, etc.) you will likely want to use these work at home tips for practice and a little spending money. For those who want something fun to do in their spare time that will make money, this is a great choice because it offers you the freedom to work as much or as little as you have time to do.

To begin, you need to build a portfolio of work to share with your potential clients. Start with some fun and even a few complex examples of what you can do. These can all be graphics you have created in your leisure time. As you build your business, you can add to that portfolio with new clients work images as they allow. Always ask before putting something on your portfolio, as some clients may want to keep things confidential.

Here are some images and items you can create for your portfolio potential clients:

- Website design

- Cartoon images for avatars and logos

- Business logos for websites, social media and business cards

- Business card and business flyer designs

- Signs and vinyl graphic designs

Once you have built your portfolio up to include examples of everything you are willing to create for your clients, you will want to create a solid price sheet. While you are still growing, you will need to be competitive in the business, but never sell yourself short. Look at competitors pricing and work within the range of what is average at that time period. Don't go too high, but don't go too low. You want your prices to reflect the quality and value of your work.

Once you are ready to begin marketing, you can look at several different places to sell your work or your services. These are just a handful of the common places you can find yourself utilized as a graphic designer.

- Submit your resume and place bids on Odesk or Elance.

- Create a Fiverr account and offer low cost graphics with upsell potential.

- Offer your services in various LinkedIn or Facebook groups for both graphic designers and virtual assistants

- Create fun basic logos to sell on stock photo websites

- Network in your local community for small business web design, business card and business flyer design

- Use your designs on vinyl graphics to sell at craft fairs, local flea markets or to businesses via Etsy, Ebay or other online sales sites.

- Blogs

I have hired both graphic designers and web designers to help complete work on my blog. Since I have no idea where to start when it comes to designing my own graphics I know how much their skills are worth and will pay accordingly. Many graphic designers do not even consider non-traditional jobs like working for a blog or websites remotely from their home.

My brother is a graphic designer and has successfully found jobs online and locally that he could complete in his free time while still working a full-time job outside of the home. As a graphic designer you normally will get paid per job and can set your own price.

EDITING & PROOFREADING

There is a wonderful niche hiding on the Internet and in publishing houses for those who have a good sense for the written word. In fact, some of them might have already been reading this and picking out small grammar errors throughout this book {sorry!}. If you are a student of the English language and are always proofreading and editing what you read online or in books then this may be the perfect job for you.

Editing the written word that is to be published in print or online includes many things. There are those who edit only for grammar and spelling errors, but there are also those who edit for fluidity and to make sure what is being read is understood by those reading it. Both of these are needed in the publishing and blogging community. If this sounds like something you would be able to do, then this chapter will be focused purely on how and where to market yourself to make money from home.

Becoming an editor or proofreader may take a bit of effort, but once you have a few happy clients under your belt the new contracts will come more easily. This is a business that does not make as much money as some other work at home business endeavors, but it is one that will give you significant flexibility, as well as give you the chance to read and learn new things on a daily basis. For the book lover out there, this is an ideal situation.

I will begin with some easy places to market your services, and then look at what it takes to build up a steady editing or proofreading business that will give you the income your family needs to succeed.

WHERE TO MARKET YOURSELF AS AN EDITOR OR PROOFREADER

One of the first places to begin offering yours services is to look at places like Odesk and Elance. These are both online virtual assistant hubs that give you the opportunity to put your resume out there for potential clients to view, as well as the chance to bid on jobs currently open. You can also consider other job forums that you can post a resume onto.

Odesk and Elance: These sites operate fairly similarly. They both require a resume submission to be on file for potential clients to view, but also allow you to bid on current job openings. While you may find individuals coming directly to you, more often than not you will find work by bidding on jobs as they are posted. Prices for your work will be exceptionally low as you will face competition from other countries that can afford to work for a much lower hourly rate. Set a minimum rate you are willing to work for, and use this as a way to create a resume of projects completed to show future clients.

Fiverr: This site is set up to allow you to offer services for the starting rate of only $5 to the buyer. You can set a word limit for the $5, and then allow yourself the opportunity to upsell for higher word counts or further products. While the initial job may feel a bit low priced, you will find good clients on fiverr that will come back again and again. Once you check out how other people are selling these types of jobs you will get a better idea of how much more you can charge for add-on jobs on this website.

LinkedIn: This social media platform is a wonderful place to showcase your skills. Not only should you have a fully completed profile, but you should join groups for freelancers, publishers, and of course editing and proofreaders.

Editing and proofreading can be a fun and easy job for those who have the natural ability to spot errors. If you are also multi-lingual, you will find even more opportunities to offer your services. Being able to proofread or edit in other languages gives you a chance to create an even more unique business model.

As you take your love of words to work with you, remember not to limit yourself. There are a multitude of ways you can work for others doing proofreading or editing. Not only for blog posts, websites or eBooks. Look into offering your skills to local college students or professors if applicable to their assignments. Offer to help go over local business websites for spelling or grammar errors in their information tabs. The places you can utilize your skills are endless.

You may not think that you can make a full-time income from editing but if you do a google search you will see how many editing and proofreading businesses there are out there. This would be a great way to work from home by doing something you enjoy.

When looking for these types of jobs you can think outside the box. You will be surprised with how many people are looking for your services.

TRANSCRIPTION

One of the most common work at home businesses is transcription. This is a great way to make money from home, but it is a business that requires some specific skills and equipment. In this section, I will cover the must have items you will need to be successful as a transcriptionist.

A transcriptionist is an individual who listens to a recording and creates a written transcription of what was recorded. The most commonly referred to instance of transcription is in regards to medical records. It is however, used in other fields including legal offices, research companies, and even telephone interviews for various businesses.

Transcriptionists are needed for a multitude of businesses, and are highly sought after. There is a high level of competition in the business, but it is a great choice for those who are great with details.

To be an effective transcriptionist, you will need to have a few set skills:

- Excellent attention to detail

- Excellent listening and retention skills

- Proficient typing skills

- Ability to multi task

- Knowledge of the information you are transcribing (not always necessary, but definitely helpful when it comes to medical terminology and spellings).

HOW TO BE A SUCCESSFUL TRANSCRIPTIONIST

The first thing you must ask yourself, is can you truly type well. I am not talking about managing 50-60 words per minute. Transcriptionists need an exceptionally high level of proficiency when typing. Your work is not paid by the word, but the amount of work you can complete in a given time frame. If you are typing at a slower rate, you will take longer to complete work thus making less per job. When tasks are due within a certain time period, it is very important to know you can complete them easily well in advance of the due date or time.

- **Have the right equipment:** Most transcriptionists will tell you that a reliable computer, good Internet provider, quality headset and a foot pedal are all that are necessary for handling the job. These items are easy to locate, and can be a relatively low investment for a new transcriptionist. You want to make sure you pay attention to the quality of your equipment. There is definitely an initial investment required for this job.

- **Have proper certification:** While being a certified transcriptionist is not necessary for many jobs, it is one way that some companies weed out applications to find those who are qualified for the job. You can invest $599-$2000 into a certificate from US Career Institute, Pen Foster or even the University of Phoenix to get a certificate saying you have been trained to be a transcriptionist. While this will not guarantee that you will land a job, it will open more doors for you. All of these programs also offer referrals to various transcription companies.

If you want to get the job, you really do have to make the right investments to become a quality transcriptionist.

WHERE TO FIND JOBS AS A TRANSCRIPTIONIST

No matter how talented you are, if you do not know where to look to find the job, you will get frustrated. Transcriptionists are used by many businesses. Some will work with you on an "as-needed" basis. Others need a daily full-time transcriptionist and you will be given set hours every day that you work. Your jobs will vary, but there is always a need for quality transcriptionists.

The places I mention here are ones that have been used by people I know. This list is not inclusive, and it does not guarantee you will get the job. It is however a great place to begin.

- **Local Physician, Hospital, Lawyer or Research Group.** Many local to you physicians, hospitals, lawyers or even research groups will hire transcriptionists for their business. Take your resume or business card into their office with a rate sheet letting them know you are available to help them out. Begin by talking to your own personal physician or lawyer to see if they need your services.

- **Tigerfish & Transcribe Me.** These sites are two of the most popular in the business. They both behave as a middle man between you and the business in search of a transcriptionist. To apply you will need to complete a speed and accuracy test. If you cannot complete the test properly, you can generally reapply after 3-6 months for a second chance with the company.

- **Odesk, Elance and Fiverr.** I know I have mentioned these over and over, but they are a wonderful resource for finding work at home jobs. All three of these are excellent options for acquiring those occasional clients that could turn into full time positions. Check out recent rates of others performing transcription through these sites and bid with comparable rates. Remember there is a lot of competition here, so work on building up your resume with quality work more than quantity of work.

Becoming a transcriptionist will require a lot of dedicated quiet time. While it is a great way to work from home and make money, it is often very difficult for those who have kids at home. The need to have complete quiet to concentrate on your job is not just important but mandatory. Any distraction can keep you from performing your work properly. This is especially important in medical and legal transcription where every word could be a life or death situation for an individual involved.

Get started preparing yourself for a future in transcription work by looking into the current options available for training, as well as looking at some of the sites mentioned above and taking practice tests.

Even though this type of work will not apply to everyone it is a legit work from home job option. Often times you can find a full-time position instead of constantly seeking work like some of the other suggestions I have already told you about in this book.

ARTS & CRAFTS

A re you an artistic individual? Do you enjoy creating beautiful artwork, clothing, jewelry or craft items? Then this section is all about how you can take a fun hobby and turn it into a full time business for yourself making money at home.

This has become one of the most popular ways for stay at home moms to make extra money for their family. Taking the things they enjoy making and doing is a great way to turn over some profit by selling them online. The arts and crafts world includes so many mediums. I am going to list some of the more popular items here for you to consider, but this is by no means everything that could be considered in this realm of product sales.

- Hand sewn clothing, bags, quilts or blankets

- Homemade decorative wreaths

- Cross stitched items, plagues and hangings

- Crocheted or knitted items like blankets, hats, scarves, gloves and shawls

- Paintings, sketches, sculptures and other hand crafted pieces of artwork

- Wood carvings

- Gift baskets, bags and other fun gift items

- Handmade jewelry or bead work

- Upcycled renovated furniture and décor items

- Homemade soaps, lotions, candles and household products

- Printable Items

- Party Decorations

WHERE TO MARKET YOUR ARTS & CRAFTS

For ultimate success with your arts & crafts business, you need to know how to get the word out to others to be able to sell your products. Below you will find some basic ideas on places and ways to get your products seen by potential customers. Before you begin marketing, however, you will want to have a few examples of your work prepared and photographed so potential customers will know what they are buying. High quality photos can be the difference between making a sale or not.

- Share on your personal social media

- Share on social media groups, swap pages and craft junkie sites. There are a ton of Facebook groups dedicated to hand crafted items. There are even auction-like options you can check out.

- Share with your local church group, MOPS group or daycare moms

- Create an Etsy shop (make sure to read all rule and regulations. Some products may not be allowed in shops due to copyright issues). This is one of the most common places I have seen people sell their handmade items. Etsy is one of the first places I turn to when I am looking for homemade items to purchase. My son's nursery has several items I bought from Etsy shop owners. Take the time to see how and what other people are selling before you jump right in.

- Create social media pages and promote in craft groups

- Attend local arts & crafts fairs, flea markets or community yard sales.

These are just a few of the places you can market your arts & crafts businesses. Depending on the products, you may want to set yourself up with a complete website for customers to make requests and special orders. Being available for your customers is key.

You really want to focus on giving not just a pretty product, but a durable product to your customers. If you want to build up clientele you want to provide quality products.

- Invest in quality supplies

- Take your time

- Test your products personally to make sure they look and work how as they are intended

- Do not be afraid to charge accordingly for higher quality products and supplies

Turn your love of crafting, or your talent for artwork into a lucrative work at home business. This type of work is specific so you may not fit into these tasks, but the types of items you can make to sell are endless. I have purchased invitations, vinyl backdrops, posters, clothing and various other items from handmade shops online. You may not think you can make money from your crafty items, but check out Easy before you rule this out as a potential source of income from home.

ONLINE AUCTIONS
& SALES WEBSITES

Many years ago before ecommerce had really become a normal concept, there was this little idea born in some persons mind called an online auction. eBay quite simply revolutionized the world of making purchases online. Our world, our habits, our hobbies and our budgets have not been the same since. Not only did this bring a collection of artwork from another country right to our living room, but it has given many individuals the perfect way to make money from home.

In this section, I am going to look at some of the ways that you can take items you currently own or can purchase through distributors and make a healthy living using online auction sites like eBay. Not only will I share with you tips on how to get your items seen by viewers, but I will look realistically at the income opportunities and how you will have to work to make a full-time income.

Gone are the get rich schemes associated with online auction sales. Reality is it can be a wonderfully business if you utilize the tools in front of you correctly.

To begin in online auction sales, you must get to know the popular sites and how they work. While there are numerous online auction sites, the most popular and one of the safest for the buyer and seller is eBay. Before you go any further, take a look around eBay so you will have an understanding of how it operates and what is offered.

HOW TO MAKE MONEY WITH eBAY

This online auction site has been around for a long time and has been one of the largest and easiest ways for individuals to make money from home that ever happened.

Learn what sells best. I am going to share some items that sell at the highest rate of turnover, and then I will show you about how you can use this knowledge to make money for yourself.

- **Collectible figurines, toys, games, books and posters.** This includes anything that is antique, in mint condition, still in original boxes or a limited edition.

- **Latest technology gadgets.** TV's, game systems, cellular phones, computers and all of the accessories that go along with them are in this category. Chargers, cases, spare parts and replacement items are all great for sales.

- **Name brand clothing.** Name brand items that still have tags on them can sell at great high prices as long as those prices are lower than in store prices. Name brand clothing that is gently used will sell at lower rates, but still bring a great rate of return and will be sought after.

- **Children's, Plus Size & Maternity Clothing.** These categories of clothing are viewed more than others. Finding good gently used items at reasonable prices is the goal. This includes things like school uniforms.

- **Books, music and DVD's.** This category can be tricky to make money from, but if you have rare or limited edition items, it is easy to sell these items at a great rate.

Once you have figured out what is popular on eBay and will make you the most money, you need to figure out how to get those sales started. Starting from scratch will be tougher to get sales when you do not have any ratings yet on eBay. However, a clear and thorough listing will give you an edge on competition.

- Post clear images of your product

- Offer free shipping on higher priced items when applicable.

- Make sure your product listings are detailed and easy to read.

- Respond to questions or comments regularly and in a timely manner.

- Post in multiple applicable categories.

- Take advantage of free listing offers, but always keep track of potential charges and fees that apply to all auctions so you can account for that in your pricing level.

Before you start selling on eBay, take the time to look at various auctions to get an idea of price ranges. If you are buying items to then resell on eBay, make sure your markup will be sufficient. Plus, it will give you a better idea of your competition and you can watch what items sell. You want to your items to be priced competitively, but you still need to make money.

I know several people who make a full-time income selling on eBay. Although it is a full-time job, you can make a nice monthly income. Even if you want to try selling items on the side to supplement your income you can make an extra thousand dollars a month depending on the items you sell.

HOW TO MAKE MONEY WITH AMAZON

I am sure when you think about Amazon you think about online shopping, but did you know that you can also sell on Amazon, too?

Selling used items that are in good condition online is a simple way to get started making money from home and Amazon is a great place to start. Some of the perks of selling on Amazon include:

- You do not need to have your own product to sell.

- You do not need to have your own website.

- You do not need to pay to promote.

- You do not need any prior experience to get started.

Selling on Amazon is simple and once you get started you will quickly learn how easy it is to make money selling on their site. Amazon does have certain fees that apply to sellers so be sure to read over their policies before jumping right in.

They will take out a percentage of the sale, but you can still double your money selling items after Amazon has taken their cut. You will not be charged any fees until your product sells.

Each time someone purchases one of your items you will receive an email from Amazon letting you know that an order has been placed. Amazon will pay you by direct deposit and will alert you as soon as a payment has been processed.

Not sure what you should sell? Amazon has over 20 categories of items that you are allowed to sell on their site, which means TONS and TONS of products. I have seen many people not only sell their used items that they have around their house, but they also purchase new items from stores or garage sales that they know will have a high profit margin.

Make sure you do your research first. Become acquainted with their site and check out the competition. Take the time to search items on their site and think of ways that you can get those items for cheaper.

Start with a few products to make sure there is a high enough profit margin for it to be worth it. Always try to double or triple your cost otherwise it will not be worth your time.

Selling on both eBay and Amazon is a great way to start to make money from item you may have sitting around in your house. You may be surprised how quickly either of these options can turn into a full-time job with a full-time income.

Making money online is not a one-time thing, and to really create secure passive income it makes sense to have multiple sources. That is why I created the Frugal Fanatic Weekly newsletter. Join our community and I will be sure to keep you up to date of the latest trends and changes of online revenue. AND you will have access to special calls, ebooks and surprises.

ONLINE CLASSIFIEDS
& SWAP SHOPS

I have already covered how online auctions work to make you money, but selling your unwanted items with online classifieds and swap shops. Craigslist has made quite a name for itself in communities as a great place to list your items for sell. Not only does it make a purchase more immediate, it can be a great way to give back to your own community. Along with Craigslist, I will look at how you can use local swap shops found on social media groups or with yahoo to make money from home.

There are definitely ways to increase the money you can make selling items you have around your house. I will share with you some great tips to help you stand out as well as provide you with the best places to look. Making money using your local classified sites and swap shops is easy when you know how to work within their guidelines.

Before you get started, evaluate what you have in your home that you would like to sell. Make a list and see how many items you can think of. Here are some ideas to get you started: books, DVD's, electronics, clothing, tools, and baby items.

If you do not have enough to have a full-fledged yard sale, then this is a great option for you. There are many people who use Craigslist and swap shop sites on a daily basis to make an income, but it is also an excellent way to get rid of items and earn money just on occasion. Whether you have a ton of stuff to get rid of, or just a few items, this information will come in handy and help you to make money from home.

HOW TO MAKE MONEY WITH CRAIGSLIST

Craigslist is a wonderful option to consider when you find unwanted items around your house to sell. Even though you may be restricted because you are only selling to local people it is much easier because you do not have to pay any shipping costs or site fees. Craigslist is separated by the closest city to where you live. You can easily list the items you want to sell after you create an account on Craigslist.

Craigslist has multiple categories for you to post in to sell items. From furniture to baby items, clothing or electronics. It is quite easily an online classified that can be used as your own personal online yard sale. Since you do not have to pay any fees to use it for posting items for sale, it is one of the easiest ways to make a great profit for your time. Plus, if the item does not sell you can wait a few weeks and try posting it again without losing any money. Before getting started take a look at their site and choose your correct city and familiarize yourself with how sales are setup.

- Read all of the site rules and regulations for each posting so you do not end up being marked as spam and removed from the site.

- Take clear pictures from all angles to include in your post. Typically 4 pictures are allowed. Items with pictures are more likely to sell than those without. Plus, it will save you time because people will see exactly what you are selling and not wasting your time by coming to see the item and not purchasing it because it was not what they had expected.

- Post items individually when applicable. Multiple pieces of furniture can be posted separately, but you can mention in each post that you have other items available.

- Put all information including general location it must be picked up in your post. Share any information about color, model, size, style, condition or any other areas that a buyer may have interest. Try to be as detailed as possible.

- Post within the right category. Make sure you are posting to the correct area of Craigslist to get the most views. People will search whole categories and if yours is not in the right place it may not show up.

- Take caution when meeting someone to make the sale. Safety is extremely important and Craigslist has a lot of scams, so take caution and meet at a public place.

When I first started selling items on Craigslist I began with small things we had around our house. Once I became familiar with the process I quickly found out how easily you can make money. There were plenty of times where I would list an item and get numerous phone calls that same day.

I cannot tell you exactly how much money you can make selling on Craigslist because it depends on what you have to sell. But, it is definitely worth trying because of how easily you can list an item without paying any fees.

HOW TO MAKE MONEY WITH SWAP SHOPS

Local swap shops can be found within Facebook or Yahoo groups. Facebook offers the easiest groups to navigate since you can include images, create albums, and promote easily throughout the day. Yahoo groups that exist are mainly handled by email and typically have more stipulations and rules. Both offer valuable ways to rid yourself of junk and make money without paying a fee like auctions sites would charge.

- Read all group regulations and abide by them. This is very important since each group will have different rules. Before posting, always make sure you have checked for rule updates just in case. The admins of these groups normally do this for free so if they see you broke a rule they will just delete you from the group because they have a lot of people to manage.

- Provide clear pictures, descriptions and information on pickup location, so potential buyers will know what they are looking at.

- Put your highest requested price so buyers have room to haggle a bit. If it sells at the highest price that is great, but if not you have comfortable room for negotiation. Everyone is always looking to get a deal so start higher than you actually want the price to be so there is room to come down without losing profit.

- Make sure items are clean and presented clearly for better chance of grabbing a buyer's attention.

- Keep track of what groups you have items posted in so you can easily update when it is pending purchase, price has lowered or it has been sold.

Local community swap shops are a great place for you to not only get rid of things like clothing, furniture and crafts, but to make extra money from home. You can also consider selling your hand crafted items in these groups as well.

DIRECT SALES
& MULTILEVEL MARKETING

This final section about real ways to make money from home is probably what could be the most popular, yet most controversial. Direct sales and multilevel marketing businesses tend to go hand in hand. They can be amazing opportunities for individuals to create a business at home around their kids, family and other obligations. However, they can be considered spammy. While you may hesitate to consider this as an actual work at home option, it is something everyone should look into because the potential earnings are much greater than some of the jobs I have told you about already.

Both direct sales and multilevel marketing programs have many perks. You can quickly start your own business with a very low investment. You are given direct access to training programs and information to help you get started and be successful. Having free training, mentors and company support for everything from your first sale to a built-in free website can be a great idea to help you kickstart your business and making money from home.

Before you write off direct sales as something that you just do not have an interest in, take a moment to look over the information in this section. Direct sales and multilevel marketing can offer you with a great home business that works around your needs and schedule.

In multilevel marketing companies you are compensated not only for the sale you generate, but also for the sales of other people that you recruit or are on your "team" or "downline". This is where the multiple levels of compensation come into play.

Direct selling is when you are marketing and selling directly to a consumer. Often times, these types of companies rely on in-home parties and one-on-one demonstrations.

A quick google search will provide you with a whole slew of choices for both multilevel marketing and direct sales companies. Some of the most popular ones include Amway, Avon, Mary Kay, doTerra and Advocare.

When I was in my first year of College I sold Avon products and was able to afford my daily living expenses, car payment, insurance and other costs that arose. I was surprised that I could support myself while in school without having to work full-time. I loved the flexibility of working around my class schedule while still making enough money to live off of and pay my bills each month.

HOW TO CHOOSE YOUR DIRECT SALES PROGRAM

When you are considering a direct sales or multilevel marketing program, you have to think about what you would feel good promoting. If you are someone who does not wear makeup, a makeup company is not a good idea for you. If you are not into fitness or health, promoting those products is not going to be good for you either. What will work is to promote and sell something you actually enjoy and appreciate.

Take some time to consider the various programs out there and what they would offer you and your family. If the program is in the startup price range you can manage, and is something you would typically buy or use anyway, then it is automatically on your radar. Sales will be much easier when you can show how you personally use the product. You are essentially endorsing the products or services you are selling so really take the time to research each company before deciding which one is best for you. Here are some tips to consider.

- Look for low startup costs that include tools you need to sell.

- Look for programs you would personally consider using or purchasing.

- Look for programs that offer personal training or mentoring during the first few months.

- Look for programs that also offer savings plans, leadership programs and potential insurance options as you increase sales.

- Take a look at their commission and compensation plans.

Choosing the right direct sales company for you is all about working with something you believe in. When you believe in what you are selling, you see much more consistent success.

HOW TO MARKET YOUR DIRECT SALES BUSINESS

This is the part that gets controversial. Marketing a direct sales or multilevel marketing business can often be considered spammy. As you look through your feed on social media, you will even find dozens of direct sales or multilevel marketing businesses being promoted. You may have hidden those in the past because you found them to be just a little bit too much. Finding the right way to market your business without going overboard is important. Here are some tips to keep in mind.

- Utilize social media to share the important developments, big sales or new product launches without posting too often. You want people to be interested without getting annoyed.

- Approach friends that you may think are interested, but do not bombard them constantly. Nothing is more frustrating than having someone constantly trying to sell their products while you are just visiting with them.

- Set up a booth at local business, craft or product fairs in your community.

- Network with others in your direct sales company to learn new promotion practices.

If you believe in your product, you can easily recommend it to everyone in your sphere of influence.

When you are just getting started figure out how you can sell you products or services. Consider making a list of all the people you know and even ask friends and family for referrals.

CONCLUSION

E ach of the jobs in this book can help you generate an income from home. Even though they may not be an easy way to make money you can learn what works best for you and work hard to build a dependable income.

As you make a decision on which of these opportunities fits your lifestyle, goals and skill set, consider the time and money you will have to invest. Understand that there are no get rich schemes out there that will bring you the millions you may want without work. You have to put in an effort to make yourself successful in any business. Here are some tips to consider now that you are ready to work from home.

- Continue the education process by taking classes, observing others and always being willing to accept constructive criticism.

- Create a dedicated time and space in your home and life to devote to business needs. That means keeping track of your paperwork, invoices, licensing and all other basic business needs. It is always best to be prepared.

- Set goals and decide which jobs will work best for you. How much money do you want or need to make? How many hours do you have to devote every day?

- When something does not work, don't give up. Try new things all the time. Ask for help from mentors and those around you who have been in the business longer.

I hope this book has given you a new insight into some great options for working from home to make real money.

Good luck!

www.ingramcontent.com/pod-product-compliance
Lightning Source LLC
Chambersburg PA
CBHW070920180526
45168CB00005B/2088